A N

(

HEAVEN

Henry Normal

INTRODUCTION

This is the seventh in a series of books.

All of the pieces were written during December '93 and January '94

DEDICATED TO DAVID AND JAN

All poems by HENRY NORMAL

Cover design by EMMA DAMON

Published by: A. K. PRESS
                 22 LUTTON PLACE
                 EDINBURGH
                 EH8 9PE

PRINTED IN GREAT BRITAIN BY UNICORN PRESS, SHEFFIELD.

A MAP
OF
HEAVEN

CONTENTS

IF SIGNATURES REFLECT PERSONALITY THEY CANNOT ALL REMAIN CONSTANT

It's not that I've forgotten my own name . . .

It's just that my signature doesn't flow naturally like it used to.

I hesitate as the pen blotches the first ink; self conscious.
Each letter has become foreign; a random code of symbols.

With deliberate forgery I have to match up my commitment with a genuine signature that has already been approved. I'm cribbing off my own past.

It's as if my signature is trying to change but is restrained by the functional need of the authorised version.

Strange how we all set our own guidelines, our own parameters so early for something so permanent. I remember practising my signature as a teenager. I'm sure I never understood this was to remain unchanged forever.

As a result my signatures have become clumsy like a child's crayon letters. I suppose I'm worried if I just sign a new signature this will not be accepted.

Is it possible to authorise a change of signature? How will I sign for it?

IN DEFENCE OF THE LATECOMER

We are all latecomers
having to pick up the threads
whilst the action continues

hastily snatching titbits of insight
from other latecomers
whose initial source was merely
better informed latecomers

informed by other latecomers
often since departed

it is a sympathetic expression of humanity
to be late
if we are not late we are not human
a latecomer is a reminder to us all of our own humanity

in a sense they offer a gesture of comradeship, however
unwitting

we should celebrate the latecomer

rejoice in our re-affirmation of a common humanity

offer them our congratulations
our thanks.

THE FIRST TIME I DIED I WAS COMPLETELY HOPELESS AT IT

The first time I died I was completely hopeless at it
As you've probably read

I'd never done it before you see
There's St Peter at the gates of Heaven
Doesn't know whether to close early for lunch or hurry me up
God's scratching his head
The Devil's re-checking his inventory
Yes . . . no . . . ?
People dying about me right left and centre not giving it a
Second thought
There's me - more trouble than I'm worth
Dithering
Stuck in some universal revolving door
Waving my arms about trying to attract attention

Am I early ?
Er . . . Shall I come back later ?
Er . . . Is there a queue ? Er . . .

Some Cherubim start to put down their harps and come to see
What all the fuss is about
Others play louder hoping I'll go away
Past relatives realising it's me skulk off
Into a blinding light
The Devil starts looking concerned and sneaks out a bottle of
Tippex

LYING ABOUT YOUR AGE

Against nature you choose to stunt progression

Devaluing yourself
Betraying new friends
You dishonour cherished moments
And demean suffering for mathematics

Instant time travel within a vacuum
You lose faith
Misalign the stars
And redraw the truth as misfit

THE 44th MINUTE

All I want now is
To be in wonder
Immersed

Reminded purity exists
Somewhere
In this universe

THE PERFECT YOU

I am the other you
the perfect you
the one bred from your DNA
taken at birth
our birth
cultivated for spare parts
kept alive by machines
and stored in the dark
waiting

We grow simultaneous
alike but not quite
for I have no defects
no scars
no scratches
no weathered skin
no blemishes
no bruises
no acquired resistance
no yellowing of the eye
no tooth decay
no furrows in the brow
no creases on the palms

no lifeline
no loveline

I am the other you
the perfect you

THE IMPERIAL PEACE MUSEUM

By the grave of the unknown civilian
Children swop Peace comics

Peace machines are glorified
As a warning

The statistics speak for themselves

There's a season of old
First World Peace films being shown
The Great Peace as it was called
Before we knew enough to allocate numbers

'You have to have lived through Peace to appreciate the full impact'
reminisces the BBC Peace correspondent

Huge armies now stand ready for the threat of Peace

It is difficult to remember a time when
Peace hasn't broken out in some corner of the world

Peace has developed its own language
Its own industry
It has become a world apart
a TV spectacle
An art bandwagon
An intellectual conundrum

And
        When the last poppy is sold
        By the last veteran
        On the last official Poppy Day
What will future generations remember
In
A world teetering on the brink of Peace ?

THE MISSING PAGE

and it made a mockery of the rest

and it became the most important of all pages

and neither of us could write a replacement

and we could never agree on its contents
        only sometimes in broad outline

and there were times when we denied it ever existed
and times when I believed it to be several pages

and it became the perfect excuse

and the amount we attributed to it could never be contained on
        a single sheet

and if only the pages had never been numbered

and

CIVIC STATUES ARE NEVER NAKED

Proud for posterity
Jaw set
Self-aware
Inactive
Like a solid photograph
This is the official face
Formal dress
Dignity without vulnerability
A permanent Sunday best
Grandeur selected to inspire
Without tenderness
Sterner than life
Humanity reduced for the importance of stonework

THE COASTER - MIGHTY BASTION OF CIVILISATION

Sponge saucer
Unsung since Chaucer

Mop twixt tea and top
Cup cop to sup up slop

Not a furnishing garnish
A guardian of the varnish
Ensuring tables free from tea stain tarnish

Diverter of drips
Leak lagging lips

O incredible
Semi-porous pedestal

Overflow screen
Go-between
Close friend of Mr Sheen

A clever gauge
To blot beverage
Of whatever age

Wedge against the wet
Ingestor of the juicy jet

The fine line against fluid anarchy
Comfort-cushion of the panicky

Epitome of order
The great absorber
Part towel part decorative plate
Absorber the great

THE DINOSAUR WAR POEMS

65 million years BC February 3rd Thursday

To Hell with the lot of them, that's what I say.
This ice age is no place for a poet.
Fight and eat, eat and fight, that's all they know.
It's like talking to an amoeba.
'We need to evolve', I told them.
'We need a thumb'.
'Warm blood', I said, 'That's the future'.
But all they do is stomp around trying to look frightening.
Nothing much happening. Went to bed early.

65 million years BC February 4th Friday

'OK let's invent fire', I said.
No response.
'What about the wheel ?'
Nothing.
We foraged around for leaves for a while.
Alan tried to charge a tree.
There was nothing we could do for him.

65 million years BC February 5th Saturday

A stegosaurus next to me in the mud is bleeding.
He's resting between bouts with a Pteradactyl.
I explained to him about air superiority.
Suggested we improve our ground to air technology.
He tried to gouge me with his horn.
I've got a bad feeling we're not going to make it.

65 million years BC February 6th Sunday

There's fierce fighting near the ravine.
No-one seems to have noticed the ice is receding.
I don't like the look of the dust that's
blowing in from the South.
Everyone's moving out.
I showed the General my plans for an 'Eco-dome'
which I believe could maintain and perpetuate a friendly
environment indefinitely.
He ate them.

65 million years BC February 7th Monday

This morning we came across a herd of creatures we had never
seen before. All of them were dead.
A couple of the older tyrannosaurs' wanted to turn back.
Fires are burning all around us now.
It's hard to tell the difference between night and day.
I can't believe there is still fighting.
The only thing that pulls me through is I know in my heart
God is on our side.

65 million years BC February 8th Thursday

I woke up sweating. No idea of the time.
I tried to find out as I have a feeling these little details
are important somehow.
Anyway the point is I'd been dreaming.
Well it was more of a nightmare really.
All I can remember was that I was dead,
and someone or something had re-assembled my bones
but had got it wrong.
I tried to correct them, diplomatically at first, but they
assured me they knew more about it than I did.
We began to fight. That's when I woke up
I'm not sure of the time. It was late, I know that.

ANIMALS AND SMALL CHILDREN FIND ME OUT

. . . it is not that I am of no worth
just that I've managed to exaggerate my worth

or at least I've allowed my worth to be exaggerated
beyond my ability to pretend justification
I don't even keep plants around the house nowadays
I had hoped to live up to this flattery

but it becomes a chore
like constantly walking round on tiptoes

and sooner or later you wonder at
the true benefit of the extra height

FOETUS MADONNA AND CHILD

Virgin birth without maternal consent

Product of a surgical rape by grave robbers

Conscripted Icon to a mutilated God

    . . . this is too impersonal

She has outgrown her parent from birth
An untidy addendum to Death's reckoning

A photo of an aborted foetus in a silver frame is no Compensation

Her nightmares would sicken even Mary Shelly

The scripture of chemical equations cannot comfort her
The strongest of nature's bonds eludes her

She could brush her grandmother in passing
And neither would ever know

The instruments of conception are kept immaculate

'Mother, I would breathe your name' she whispers

The victim Madonna

In sterile hands
She is no bigger than a doner card

I SET MY WATCH 30 MINUTES FAST THIS MORNING AND WATCHED MYSELF SLEEP A WHILE

I set my watch 30 minutes fast this morning
And watched myself sleep a while

Touching the edges of the universe
Others existing only in dreams

I pulled back the curtains
And witnessed the world coping without me

All day
I caught the change in people as I entered their lives

Saw how they behaved differently before I arrived
It was if I was watching them sleeping

Tomorrow I'll set my watch back an hour to see how other edges
Close in as I leave

See myself as ghost in other dreams

DANCING WITH THE TRUTH

Body Language being somewhat uncouth
Movement exposes an inner truth

Such subtleties of posture being beyond our perception
We are not yet truly adept at dance deception

So Politicians should have to choreograph their speeches
The Bossa Nova should be made compulsory for teachers

Job interviews should be set to ballet
Freud replaced by Gene Kelly

Priests should practise pirouettes at the altar
The news should be read by John Travolta

Come Dancing should replace the United Nations
With Fred Astaire the model for diplomatic relations

The National Anthem replaced by the Lambada
A Strictly Ballroom channel should replace Granada

The Police should enforce the Foxtrot
Criminals sentenced to Tango alone on the spot

The big bands brought back
            to replace the military drummer
The only Twist
        being like that
                    that we did last summer

THE MERCURIAN LOVE POEMS

Now no time   love poems
Wrap   pages   your arms
Across   blisters

God   good, we   together

Try not swallow   too often
    lend you   shadow,   must dig

See   leg bleed
Smear   blood   your face

    must not
    cry again
        so soon

Lay beneath   body   is moisture lost to   ground

    would touch   but for   pain

These   only words, let   breath cool face

When   happens   must not give up

Stretch   over you, wear me like   outer skin

THE QUEEN'S ENGLISH

a bit of Latin when chattin'
goes down a stormer
pro forma

so always use a foreign word or phrase
remember one is never ill one has a malaise

one never has a cross word always a fracas
and never together but always en masse

fair exchange is quid pro quo
one never goes outdoors but alfresco

use adieu instead of farewell
never bathe nude always au naturel

never throw a party always a soirée
it is enough to be au fait per se

be particular in the words you use
never have meetings but rendezvous

as the piéce de résistance remember if the Queen calls up
one can forgive a faux pas but never a balls up

DOES THE MAGICIAN BELIEVE IN MAGIC?

What is the magic when the trick is known?

is it the effect of the trick?
is that enough?

or the mere existence of the trick?
the act of its invention?

or the guarding of its secret?

or that a world exists in which magic is possible
in which magic is held in wonderment?

is there magic for which there are no tricks?

or only tricks yet to be uncovered?

CUPID'S PIN CUSHION

Struck by Cupid's bow
My heart is lack lustre
I've been hit by more arrow
s than General Custer

LATE NIGHT IMPROVISED EUPHEMISTIC VALENTINE

Roses are red
Violets are less so
Do you want coffee
Ground or espresso?

IS RED THE COLOUR OF PASSION?

Roses are red
Not so the dahlia
But after sex
You can include genitalia

THE FLORIST AND THE BUTCHER

Amid new life she skips
In death his grip is strong
She gives him her tulips
He give her his tongue

LIKE A TELEPHONE VOICE YOU HAVE
PERFECTED A PHOTO FACE

For this is

the self conscious playing of you
the you the world at large are told to remember
the you with headlights on full beam at the oncoming traffic
the you to whom you feel you must aspire
the auditioning of you
the outside you
the heightened shell
the bold hoardings
the you without doubt or hesitation
the party you

None of your photos do you justice

THE PRECISE DEFINITION OF WHAT CONSTITUTES POETRY

DWARF - (ANGRILY) We'd like a word with you Snow White.

SNOW WHITE - What's the matter Happy ?

DWARF - I'm not happy.

SNOW WHITE - Why of course you are.

2nd DWARF - Wash your ears out stupid, he says he's not.

SNOW WHITE - Why Bashful, what's up with you today ?

2nd DWARF - What's up. I'll tell you what's up. We're sick of being typecast, that's what's up.

DWARF - Have you ever tried being happy 24 hours a day, seven days a week ?

SNOW WHITE - I never thought.

3rd DWARF - And she calls me Dopey.

SNOW WHITE - Not you as well Dopey ?

3rd DWARF - It's not Dopey anymore, it's Nigel.

SNOW WHITE - But I thought your names suited your characters.

4th DWARF - I haven't sneezed in months, OK I had a bad cold once and I sneezed a few times. It went to my chest after a week and I was coughing up blood but did anyone call me Chesty? Am I to be labelled forever for one lousy summer cold ?

5th DWARF - You think you've got problems. How am I supposed to get a job with a name like Sleepy ?

SNOW WHITE - Well it's just as bad for me. I'm just as typecast as you. We are all just shorthand images conjured up by a stock interpretation of scant markings. Anyway, what's Grumpy got to say about it all ?

DWARF - Oh you know Grumpy, he'll go along with anything.

IT IS DIFFICULT TO MEASURE A LIVE SNAKE

To measure the weight of a live snake
you hold it
and step onto the scales
measuring both yourself and the snake

then you measure yourself
and subtract that from the total

the difference is the snake

To measure the length
of a live snake
is more difficult

and hardly seems worth the effort

what does it matter if its longer
or shorter than another snake

does it matter even to another snake
or the snake itself

When dead
the snake may be measured and dissected or made to wear
a silly hat if required

But a live snake is a more difficult proposition

MEDICAL RECORDS OF THE LOVE SICK

CHAPTER ONE -
MAYBE THEY SHOULD TEACH SEX EDUCATION AT
SUNDAY SCHOOL

I spent all my pocket money buying her religious memorabilia.

It's not that either of us were particularly religious. Church trips were merely a cheap day out.

These gifts were tokens of love, prizes, favours, offerings.

Not being able to afford a substantial amount to demonstrate my passion I even slipped in a couple of extra non-purchased acquisitions; religious texts and novelty items. I was stealing from God.

On reflection, I don't recall receiving any keepsakes in return.

However, at the time, I was oblivious to such a technicality.

My heart was overflowing with the need to give myself. All of myself and that being not enough, to give more. To sacrifice myself. My every possession, my every principle, my immortal soul. Regretting that I only had one immortal soul to give and that it wasn't bigger.

And for what ? For reciprocal worship ? No this was more than I could hope. Like asking God himself to budge up a bit. No, unconsciously I had settled at a lesser ambition. I had settled for the chance to be allowed to worship.

SITTING ON THE IDEA OF GRASS

Sitting on grass
worms writhe in wet soil only a breath beneath the surface
insects inch between the blades

this is not the idea of grass upon which you're sitting

of village cricket and croquet on the lawn
of parasols and summer picnics
of green carpets and rose gardens

Eating cheese
it is not the view through the microscope you are eating

Admiring a body
it is not the tissue and fibres, the bones and the organs you
hold in mind

Falling in love
you select your level of perception

FOR THOSE WHO FIND THE MALE ORGAN THREATENING

Consider the male sex organ as a wooden spoon.

The wooden spoon is rigid but non-threatening. No one is ever battered or murdered by a wooden spoon.

Considered neither bawdy nor phallic in the heroic/epic sense it is free from the usual legacy of cheeky double-entendre or macho posturing.

It is a commonplace object used mainly around the house. It may not be the stuff of romantic fiction but it is practical and its connotations are more in keeping with the true nature of sex.

Essentially domestic it is easy to grip, rounded and blunt and is used to best effect on special occasions.

The metaphor of cake-making may not seem at first the most masculine of images to excite your gastric juices but the expertise of the master chef is in no way considered effeminate.

Working in a slow circular motion the wooden spoon is ideal for softening and stirring. With the addition of moisture a gradual and sustained increase in the whipping motion can produce satisfactory results. Licking the spoon is perhaps not to everyone's taste.

THE JOY OF FROGS

Frogs need kisses like anyone else

Not all of them want to become handsome Princes
Some prefer a more pond-based lifestyle

What if you turn into a handsome Prince and the Princess really
Prefers frogs?

What if you're not that handsome a Prince ?
Maybe you're more handsome a frog ?

Let's face it, chances are
If you can get kissed fairly regularly by a Princess
And remain a frog
You've got it made

If she gives you tongues
Then go for it

MISS FEBRUARY

Least famous of the dozen

She is not evident to promote sales like January
To some she is the first disappointment of the calendar

She does not offer Optimism or Resolve with the
Freshness of a truly clean sheet

She does not promise new life with the
Same authority as her replacement

She is never sure how she should be clothed
    The best winter costumes having already been modelled
    The spring collection held back
There is a feeling of making up the numbers

February is a corridor of a month

Leap year she smiles that extra smile
But it is the fleeting smile of a receptionist
Or a cloakroom attendant

RECOVERED FRAGMENTS OF THE DIDSBURY SCROLLS (TRANSLATED)

1. Believed to be a vision of New York or similar large city with skyscrapers and an airport

head upon head
silver ladders
hard mud forest sleeps a mirror constellation
the setting apart of humming stones
plague cemetery overgrown with the drinking of tears
mites and fireflies sharing nests

2. Regarded as perhaps a reference to cars and motorways

a thousand stallions harnessed
hungry dog dragging its cage
across charcoal parchment
mercury loose   in scorched guttering

3. Generally agreed to predict Power stations and electricity

monasteries of grey hair
scalding alters baptized

breaking of a child's breath
screaming core of infant sun
tiny rivers of flame
smacking the sleeping and the dead

4. A suggestion of trains and train lines maybe?

habitual snakes
companion paths of dullened beams
soil edge gentle curve

5. Modern warfare as seen on TV is the experts guess

daggers spat in anger
sticks breaking like trees
death beneath the heaven cross
witnesses all   in solid candles
                      growling corners

6. Photographs?

       likenesses and markings stiff
       moment cards trapped by size
stationary reflections
frosted memory

7. Telephones?

       sleeping cat chained to walls
stealing voices for   whispers

8. Difficult to interpret. Factories being the current favourite.

songs of long pain
grooming the inners out
tribal worship of impatient digestion
ritual bowing
               the weathering of muscle

9. Computers?

       the counting of sand
glove for the seasons change
      numbered milk pulsing eye

THE HEART OF THE LAST MAMMOTH

Not even on prime time TV
But on the minority interest channel
I saw a scientist break open the heart of a mammoth
'It is very rare' he said
'There are only two in existence'

We were never told if
The other mammoth's heart
Had yet been broken

DOES ART IMITATE ETERNAL LIFE ?

Why do we picture
The Adam and Eve of scripture
With a stomach button
If neither
Adam nor Eve were
Born of woman?

Is religious art falsely inspired
To portray Adam so abdominally attired?

Is it unthinking aesthetic
Clumsy cosmetic
Prematurely generic
Profane or prophetic?

At no point did the word of the Lord
Mention the tying of an umbilical cord
Adam is therefore unable
To have had a navel
As only those from Eve begotten
Should receive a stomach button

An interpretation
I would proffer in the artist's defence
Was that the God of creation
Gave birth to Adam in the physical sense

Or that Adam being made in his image, The Almighty
Has a similar skin dimple under his nightie

Two conclusions thus prevail
From this anatomical omen
God is either female,
Or was born of a woman

THE THIRD TESTAMENT OF ADVERTISING

Create a famine
Place the product

Tattoo the naked and the starving
Record their dying breath for the voice-over
Sell advertising space on gravestones

Sponsor a war
The firm's name on every bullet

Criminalise private grief
Hidden cameras at every funeral

Disease a spectator sport
Torture a game show

Change your title to Mushroom Cloud
And drop an atomic bomb as a gimmick

Outbid The Church of Coke
The Benetton bible
Put the Buddah on Slimcea

Coin the slogan
Re-crucify Christ on a Macdonald's sign
Over 20 million souls saved

THE LOST GENERATION OF MERMEN AND MERMAIDS

I've flushed most of my descendants down the loo
Unconsummated angels on clouds of tissue

I have squandered over five billion emissaries
En route to fertile ovaries

Wasted another five million destination unknown
Stunting their growth much more than my own

Whole cemeteries of condoms I've created
Non starters not begat but now belated

The dumped diehard deliverers of DNA
Trashed tadpole triggers of the family way

Minute Duncan Goodhues that got no further
Than gossamer graves and milky mass murder

Cul-de-sac germination
Timely entrapment and termination

A self induced final solution
Ethnic cleansing of my own evolution

THE OTHER SIDE OF THE CONVERSATION

She never really believed intelligent life existed
On the other side of the conversation

There were of course lulls in her speech pattern
Intermittent respites

These grew shorter
As her preoccupation with self-expression grew

She had become so obsessed with
Emitting encoded distress signals

She had failed to notice when
Gradually her antenna had fallen into disrepair

Recently she has taken to shouting at distant objects
Her own diction becoming garbled
Data without cohesion

Her assumptions about the universe have since become based on
Superstition

She has ignored all outside attempts to communicate
She has taken to fighting abstract concepts

Exploring inner space

EXAGGERATED THOUGHTS ABOUT AN INTERNAL BRUISE

There's a figure took to sitting on my bed at night.
I've asked him if he's me
and he says he thinks not.

I've asked him what he symbolises then
and he says he's not sure he symbolises anything.

I've asked him what he's doing there
and he says he's been wondering that himself.

I've asked him if he knows how long he plans to stop
and he says it's difficult to make any plans when you only
exist intermittently and in another's imagination at that.

I've asked him if he's one of those ominous dark brooding
shadows that appear in poetry purporting to be deep and
meaningful
but he just looked at me in disbelief and said he bloody hoped not.

My girlfriend refuses to discuss him. She's never seen him.
He's never there when she stops.

He was there once when I lived with my old girlfriend but we
broke up a week later.

I seem to remember first seeing him when I was about ten or
eleven. Around Christmas time. Of course, he was a lot younger
then.

He mostly confines himself to the bedroom. Although I have seen
him once or twice out of the corner of my eye sat on the bus.
And last summer I could have swore he was following me
everywhere I walked.

There's not a lot more to say about him really. He keeps
himself to himself. He tries very hard not to appear ominous
and gets quite embarrassed if you mention it.

SIX COUPLETS IN NEED OF DEVELOPMENT

1. On confessional poetry

There are no skeletons in my cupboard
Only strange foodstuffs I tend to hoard

2. On the subjective nature of empathy

Who really gives a toss
About the pain of a wasp?

3. On the racist who can speak so tenderly about the birth of a child

Even the most brutish
Has a sense of honour and duty

4. On the difficulty of reality living up to over-sentimental expectations

Home is where the heart is
But 2 hours later and you're looking for an excuse to leave

5. On the the redistribution of atoms and the repetition of history

Some breathe in Hitler
Whilst others breathe a saviour

6. On the anticipation of regret

As soon as the flight leaves your finger tips
You know if the target is missed

A MAP OF HEAVEN

Baythorn Rd

I am stood at the gate with my two younger sisters. I am 13. It
is about a year after my mum died. We all still have blonde
hair. The picture is a little hazy. In the background you can
see our council house and the council house behind it and the
council house behind that. We are in front of the front door.
The hedge and the roses are growing wild. Valerie and Angela
are in bathing costumes so I suppose it must be summer. My
Aunty Margaret is just about visible on the edge of the
picture.

Seaside

My sister Angela holds her windmill against the breeze. The
caravans are positioned like a council estate by the sea. The
grass is as wild as our front lawn. Our caravan is right next
to the beach. I have on grey socks and school plimsolls. At the
far end of the prom is the fun-fair. There are a few clouds but
the wind is quite strong. My cheap football is too light to
play in these conditions.

Show ground

The sun is in our eyes. We have one hand each around the others'
middle. We are both looking forward with the same daft grin.
Sally has a streak of grey in her hair and carries a couple of
bags. My feet are totally lost. We are positioned such that the
two cars behind only show one headlight each. If it was in fact
one car the arrangement would be ok, if somewhat mismatched.

Registery office

We are kissing. A light behind us gives Sally a halo. A plant
at her back gives the impression of nature providing her wings.
I am in a cheap suit with a thick knotted tie. My medium long
hair and sideburns suggest a bygone fashion. The background is
functional but antiseptic. Our eyes are closed, we are holding
hands, our lips touching. Two phones lie dormant.

Countryside

I'm the ass on the right. I only appear to be leaning on the
horse. In truth I hardly touch it at all. I'm not really
dressed for the countryside. My Western-style slightly flared
jeans and chequered shirt are off set by my black suit jacket.
The jacket was a nod in the direction of Groucho Marx in 'Go
West' but only in my own imagination. My ex-wife's shadow is
moving across the soil. My head is in a different field.

Bench

I am sat between my two younger sisters on a bench at Wollaton
Park. We are in front of the summerhouse and it is the week I
give up Insurance to become a writer. Both my arms and my legs
are crossed but I'm leaning way back on the seat. Both sisters
have their arms around my shoulders. There are flowers visible
through the glass.

Back to back

The sunlight on the brickwork extenuates my deep-set eyes. This
is the back of a back-to-back. My head is framed in the window.
I am standing under an empty line. The wall is half-painted.
There is an attempt at a garden on one side of me but without
any sign of life. On the other side children's toys are in
shadow. A white towel hangs ready.

Church

This looks very posed. I'm stood by the church I used to attend
as a child. The gates are locked. It is run down. My sister's
unsteady hand gives the building a strange outline. To try and
get in the top of the edifice my sister has to kneel. My hair
is badly cut. I'm looking directly into camera, my hands behind
my back like a naughty choir boy.

Beach

Me on a beach collecting shells. I am framed kneeling in the
top left corner. My head is cut off just above the hairline.
The photo is slightly discoloured as though looking through
rose coloured spectacles. This gives the impression my face is
sun tanned. My white calfs probably show a truer colour. I'm
wearing narrow-leg jeans and a German ex-army shirt. A comb is
just about discernible in my back pocket. Although my body
posture is away from camera I'm turning to acknowledge the
lens.

Stage

I am reading a poem I have written on the back of a baked beans
label. It is a very small stage. I'm performing at a college
during the lunch hour. I've not taken my coat off. I have a
file for my poems from a paper firm. It says 'fine papers'. My
head seems to almost touch the ceiling. There is only one light
in the distance.

Punk club

My arms are raised across a banner proclaiming 'Substitute Flesh'. An ironing board, an alarm clock and a hoover seem out of place amongst the guitars. My sleeves are rolled up and there is a man behind me with a stick. My tie is tucked into my shirt in military fashion. A duck is leant against the floral wallpaper.

Pop concert

It's an outside stage. I'm beating out time on two drum sticks. My hair is dyed. Behind me there is a man very noticeable in a camouflage jacket. The stage is red. A man in a red shirt watches my conduct at the mike.

School

I'm dressed all in black wearing 3D glasses, my hair defying gravity. I'm leading the assembly in a joke prayer. School children are laughing. There is an empty seat beside me. Outside the sun is shining. The exit is obstructed.

Manchester

This is one of my professional photo faces. The picture is in black and white and my costume is chosen to help produce the contrast. My raised eye brows furrow my forehead. The microphone is not plugged in it is just a prop. It is held to my cheek obscuring one of my dimples. My mouth seems tightly controlled, my collar not quite done up.

A HAPPY ENDING (REVISED)

. . . and they all lived happily ever after.

Well not all. Not all the time that is.

You've got to remember the book may have taken four or five
hours to read but its story was meant to span several years.
They obviously picked out the main action and discarded the
mundane. You know, the trips to the toilet, the coming back to
close the curtains, the days when someone wasn't feeling very
clever so they just took it easy...that sort of stuff.

So when it says 'they all lived happily ever after' you have to
take it as read there'd still be days, even weeks when nothing
much happened. Someone might get a bit bored or feel a bit so
so about an idea. Someone else might feel tired all of a sudden
or feel that life was becoming repetitive, or passing them by.

The film was only an hour fifteen which meant they missed out a
lot of the book. They even spiced up a few scenes to enhance
the action.

So when it says 'they all lived happily ever after'
they meant
that on the whole
given the human condition
they had a relatively happy existence
remembering that they'd got over the worst of the bad stuff
during the making of the story,
forming as it did the basis of the plot
and given that we left the main characters on a high
as is the nature of romanticised story telling leading to such
an obviously flawed generalisation.

DOES A BAD CURTAIN CALL RUIN A SHOW ?

I'm never any good at goodbye's . . .

I feel too much pressure to produce some sort of fitting
climax. As though fulfilling a duty or observing the
constraints of an art form.

It's the unalterable finality I feel looming like a punchline
you know is not going to work. A polite thankyou and goodnight
never seems sufficient. We expect . . .

He'll pull something from up his sleeve you'll see. It'll end
with a bang. The big finale. It's not over till the fat lady
sings. He'll have held something special back. Always save the
best till last. Wait for the fireworks. There's bound to be
fireworks.

I'm stood at the door again, having said all I've got to say,
having had a great time, nervous that I could spoil it all in 3
seconds. Am I the only one who feels there's too much onus on
the notion of climax? Am I lacking in stamina, character,
goodwill?

Are people so fickle that the last thing you say colours every
other gesture?

Are peoples memories so short they cannot cast their minds back
to five or ten minutes before the end?

I can never kiss that much more than I kissed at the height of
my passion. I can never wave that better wave, exert that extra
effort, surpass everything that's gone before.

So a thankyou and goodnight will have to suffice.

Of course, if I do happen to make a grand exit
two minutes later I have to return,
having forgotten my hat . . .

POETRY BY HENRY NORMAL NOW IN PRINT -

A MORE INTIMATE FAME
A5 Book 116 pages, 4 colour laminated cover, bound. Cover design by
Emma Damon. Compilation of first 3 books; Is Love Science Fiction?
Love Like Hell and Does Inflation Affect the Emotions?
ISBN 1 871426 60 X Twist in the Tale Price £6.00

THE DREAM TICKET (Second Edition)
A5 Book 52 pages, 4 colour laminated cover, bound. Cover design by
Emma Damon. Revised 4th collection
ISBN 1 873176 31 7 A.K. Press Price £4.80

THE FIFTEENTH OF FEBRUARY (Second Edition)
A5 Book 52 pages, 4 colour laminated cover, bound. Cover design by
Emma Damon. Revised 5th collection
ISBN 1 873176 41 4 A.K. Press Price £4.80

THE THIRD PERSON
A5 Book 56 pages, 4 colour laminated cover, bound. Cover design by
Emma Damon. 6th collection
ISBN 1 873176 36 8 A.K. Press Price £4.80

A MAP OF HEAVEN
A5 Book 52 pages, 4 colour laminated cover, bound. Cover design by
Emma Damon. 7th collection
ISBN 1 873176 62 7 A.K. Press Price £4.80

NUDE MODELLING FOR THE AFTERLIFE
A5 Book 72 pages, 4 colour laminated cover, bound. Cover design by
Jane Lewis. A selected works from first 6 collections
ISBN 1 85224 279 5 Bloodaxe Books Price £5.95

Available from all good bookshops
and direct from:

A.K. Distribution,
22 Lutton Place,
Edinburgh
EH8 9PE
Tel/Fax 031 6671507

(include 60p p&p and
allow 14 days for delivery)

SOME RECENT TITLES FROM AK PRESS

BAD
James Carr with an introduction by Dan Hammer
ISBN 1 873176 21 X; 224pp, two colour cover, perfect bound, 6" x 9"; £5.95/$7.95
"When I was 9 years old I burned down my school." So begins the searing autobiography of a former child prodigy of crime in the streets of LA's ghettos. He relates his story with cold passion, illuminating daily life on the streets and in prison. First published and banned in 1975, this is its first reprinting.

TESTCARD F: TELEVISION, MYTHINFORMATION AND SOCIAL CONTROL
constructed by anonymous
ISBN 1 873176 91 0; 80pp, four colour cover, perfect bound, 5½" x 8½"; £4.50/$6.00
Using savage image-text cut and paste, this book explodes all previous media theory and riots through the Global Village, looting the ideological supermarket of all its products.

END TIME: NOTES ON THE APOCALYPSE
G A Matiasz
ISBN 1 873176 96 1; 320pp, four colour cover, perfect bound, 5½" x 8½"; £5.95/$7.00
A first novel by G A Matiasz, an original voice of slashing thought-provoking style.
"A compulsively readable thriller combined with a very smart meditation on the near-future of anarchism. *End Time* proves once again that Sci-Fi is our only literature of ideas." — Hakim Bey.

NO PITY
Stewart Home
ISBN 1 873176 46 5; 144pp, mono cover, perfect bound, 5½" x 8½"; £5.95/$12.95
With this collection of 9 short stories, Mr Home gives fiction back the bad name it deserves.

STEALWORKS
THE GRAPHIC DETAILS OF JOHN YATES
John Yates
ISBN 1 873176 51 1; 136pp, two colour cover, perfect bound, 8½" x 11"; £7.95/$11.95
A collection to date of work created by a visual mechanic and graphic surgeon. His work is a mixture of bold visuals and minimalist to-the-point social commentary, involving the manipulation and re-interpretation of culture's media imagery.

AK Press publishes and distributes – to trade and retail – a wide variety of radical literature. For our latest catalogue, featuring these and several thousand other titles, please send a large self-addressed, stamped envelope to:

AK Press
22 Lutton Place
Edinburgh, Scotland
EH8 9PE, Great Britain

AK Press
PO Box 40682
San Francisco, CA
94140-0682